ath Park

Rover Way

Newport Road

Tremorfa Park

ADAMSDOWN

Moorland Park

SPLOTT

CUM

LL

WELSH ASSEMBLY

Roath Dock

G

Queen Alexandra Dock

N
W   E
S

Key

Church

School

Information

Fire station

Train station

Bus station

D0279758

Welsh Assembly | Millennium Stadium | Pierhead Building | Cardiff Castle | National Museum Cardiff | Llandaff Cathedral | University | St David's Hall

HOMETOWN HISTORY

DIFF

SUE BARROW

HOMETOWN WORLD

I helped defeat Iestyn ap Gwrgan. Read about me on page 10.

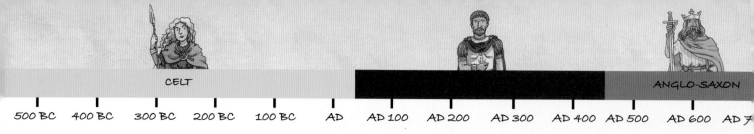
How well do you know your town?

Have you ever wondered what it would have been like living in Cardiff when the Romans arrived? What about rubbing shoulders with the finest people in the land in Cardiff Castle? This book will uncover the important and exciting things that happened in your town.

Want to hear the other good bits? You will love this book! Some rather brainy folk have worked on it to make sure it's fun and informative. So what are you waiting for? Peel back the pages and be amazed at what happened in your town.

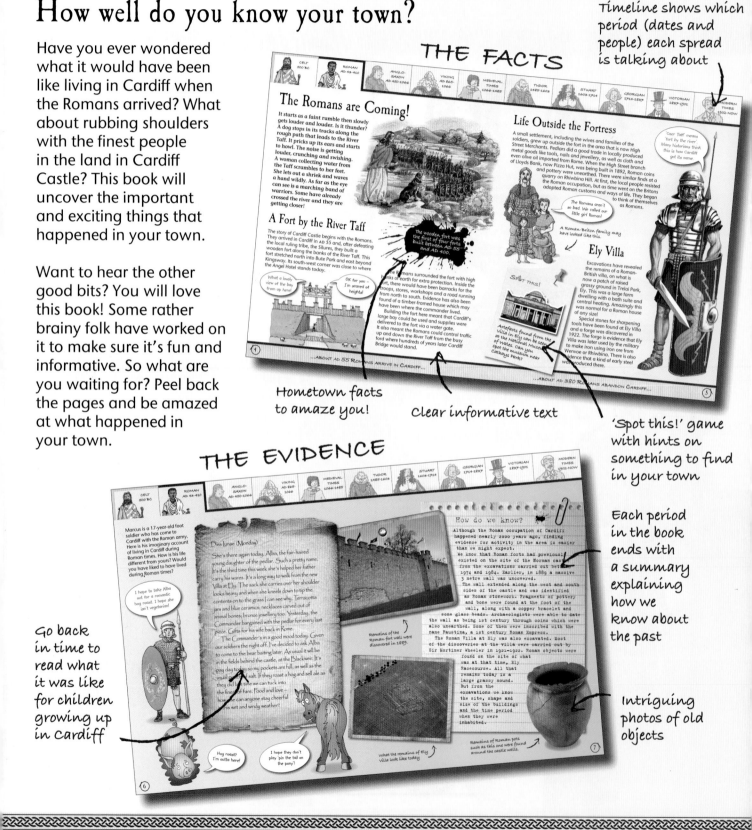

Timeline shows which period (dates and people) each spread is talking about

Hometown facts to amaze you!

Clear informative text

'Spot this!' game with hints on something to find in your town

Each period in the book ends with a summary explaining how we know about the past

Go back in time to read what it was like for children growing up in Cardiff

Intriguing photos of old objects

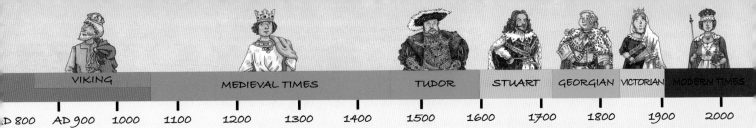

Contents

CELT
500 BC

ROMAN
AD 43–410

ANGLO-
SAXON
AD 450–1066

VIKING
AD 865–
1066

MEDIEV
TIME.
1066–1

The Romans are Coming!

It starts as a faint rumble then slowly gets louder and louder. Is it thunder? A dog stops in its tracks along the rough path that leads to the River Taff. It pricks up its ears and starts to howl. The noise is getting louder, crunching and swishing. A woman collecting water from the Taff scrambles to her feet. She lets out a shriek and waves a hand wildly. As far as the eye can see is a marching band of warriors. Some have already crossed the river and they are getting closer!

A Fort by the River Taff

The story of Cardiff Castle begins with the Romans. They arrived in Cardiff in AD 55 and, after defeating the local ruling tribe, the Silures, they built a wooden fort along the banks of the River Taff. This fort stretched north into Bute Park and east beyond Kingsway. Its south-west corner was close to where the Angel Hotel stands today.

The wooden fort was the first of four forts built between AD 55 and AD 400.

What a lovely view of the bay from up here!

OK for you – I'm scared of heights!

The Romans surrounded the fort with high banks of earth for extra protection. Inside the fort, there would have been barracks for the troops, stores, workshops and a road running from north to south. Evidence has also been found of a timber-framed house which may have been where the commander lived.

Building the fort here meant that Cardiff's large bay could be used and supplies were delivered to the fort via a water gate. It also meant the Romans could control traffic up and down the River Taff from the busy ford where hundreds of years later Cardiff Bridge would stand.

...ABOUT AD 55 ROMANS ARRIVE IN CARDIFF...

Life Outside the Fortress

A small settlement, including the wives and families of the soldiers, grew up outside the fort in the area that is now High Street. Merchants and pedlars did a good trade in locally produced metal goods like tools, nails and jewellery, as well as cloth and even olive oil imported from Rome. When the High Street branch of Lloyds Bank, now Pizza Hut, was being built in 1892, Roman coins and pottery were unearthed. There were similar finds at a quarry on Rhiwbina Hill. At first, the local people resisted the Roman occupation, but as time went on the Britons adopted Roman customs and ways of life. They began to think of themselves as Romans.

'Caer Taff' means 'fort by the river'. Many historians think this is how Cardiff got its name.

The Romans aren't so bad. We called our little girl Roman!

A Roman-Briton family may have looked like this.

Ely Villa

Excavations have revealed the remains of a Roman-British villa, on what is now a patch of raised grassy ground in Trelai Park, Ely. This was a large farm dwelling with a bath suite and central heating. Amazingly this was normal for a Roman house of any size!

Special stones for sharpening tools have been found at Ely Villa and a forge was discovered in 1922. The forge is evidence that Ely Villa was later used by the military to make iron using iron ore from Wenvoe or Rhiwbina. There is also evidence that a kind of early steel was produced there.

SPOT THIS!

Artefacts found from the Villa in Ely can be seen at the National Museum of Wales. Can you spot the museum near Cathays Park?

Marcus is a 17-year-old foot soldier who has come to Cardiff with the Roman army. Here is his imaginary account of living in Cardiff during Roman times. How is his life different from yours? Would you like to have lived during Roman times?

> I hope to take Alba out for a romantic hog roast. I hope she isn't vegetarian!

Dies Lunae (Monday)

She's there again today, Alba, the fair-haired young daughter of the pedlar. Such a pretty name. It's the third time this week she's helped her father carry his wares. It's a long way to walk from the new Villa at Ely. The sack she carries over her shoulder looks heavy and when she kneels down to tip the contents on to the grass I can see why. Terracotta jars and blue ceramics; necklaces carved out of animal bones; bronze jewellery too. Yesterday, the Commander bargained with the pedlar for every last piece. Gifts for his wife back in Rome.

The Commander's in a good mood today. Given our soldiers the night off. I've decided to ask Alba to come to the bear baiting later. As usual it will be in the fields behind the castle, at the Blackweir. It's pay day today so my pockets are full, as well as getting the usual pouch of salt. If they roast a hog and sell ale as they did last time we can tuck into the finest of fare. Food and love – how else can anyone stay cheerful in this wet and windy weather?

> Hog roast? I'm outta here!

> I hope they don't play 'pin the tail on the pony'!

TUDOR
1485-1603

STUART
1603-1714

GEORGIAN
1714-1837

VICTORIAN
1837-1901

MODERN
TIMES
1902-NOW

Remains of the
Roman fort wall were
discovered in 1889.

How do we know?

Although the Roman occupation of Cardiff happened nearly 2000 years ago, finding evidence for activity in the area is easier than we might expect.

We know that Roman forts had previously existed on the site of the Norman castle from the excavations carried out between 1974 and 1984. Earlier, in 1889 a massive 3 metre wall was uncovered. The wall extended along the west and south sides of the castle and was identified as Roman stonework. Fragments of pottery and bone were found at the foot of the wall, along with a copper bracelet and some glass beads. Archaeologists were able to date the wall as being 1st century through coins which were also unearthed. Some of them were inscribed with the name Faustina, a 1st century Roman Empress.

The Roman Villa at Ely was also excavated. Most of the discoveries at the villa were carried out by Sir Mortimer Wheeler in 1921-1922. Roman objects were found on the site of what was at that time, Ely Racecourse. All that remains today is a large grassy mound. But from the excavations we know the site, shape and size of the buildings and the time period when they were inhabited.

What the remains of Ely
Villa look like today.

Remains of Roman pots
such as this one were found
around the castle walls.

Raiders and Settlers

A shout goes up. A ship is sighted. The children and men run towards the shore. The boys shout excitedly, they have never seen such strange boats. The women, breathless with fear, have caught them up. Some men have left the ships and are running towards their land, carrying swords and shields. The women fall to their knees, praying to God to spare them from these invaders.

The Anglo-Saxon Threat

About 1,600 years ago when the Romans were still in control, warring tribes from north-western Europe, called Anglo-Saxons, began to invade parts of Britain. They were pagan people who believed in war as a way of gaining land and slaves. Although there are no records of these sea raiders in Glamorgan, there would have been great fear among the local people. To protect themselves they built hill forts.

The most important defence in the area was at Dinas Powis, south-west of Cardiff. Here a hill fort from the Iron Age was reoccupied during the 5th and 6th centuries. The South Wales coastline came under threat again 300 years later, this time from Viking raiders. They raided but did not settle in Cardiff. It wasn't until the Normans arrived that life in Cardiff really changed.

Us Vikings may look fierce but really we're all hair!

← Llandaff Cathedral today.

Monastery at Llandaff

In the same period, missionaries from Ireland, Scotland, France and Wales were converting people from paganism to Christianity. A monastery established at Llandaff is thought to be one of the earliest church sites in Britain. Many people believe that its founder was St Teilo who came from West Wales to Llandaff in about AD 560. No remains have survived, but from other monasteries like it we know that in the centre there would have been a very small church surrounded by a group of huts for the monks, enclosed by the wall of the 'llan' (settlement).

...ABOUT AD 450 ANGLO-SAXONS SETTLE IN BRITAIN...

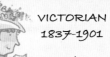

Most Anglo-Saxons were pagans which meant they worshipped a different god for every area of life.

How do we know?

To know what went on in Anglo-Saxon times we have to rely on written records and the small number of sites where remains have been found. We know about the hill forts because of archaeological excavations. Interestingly wine jars and continental pottery were found at the Dinas Powis site. This shows that although there was little organised business, and towns did not develop at this time, some trade was still being carried on between this part of Wales and Mediterranean lands.

Usually, the only people who could read and write in Anglo-Saxon times were monks and other churchmen. One of the most important accounts of the early church in Llandaff was written by St Chad in the 8th century. His account is sometimes called the Book of Gospels, but is better known as the Book of St Chad. It was written in old Welsh and another ancient language. Another remarkable relic of this time is the Book of Llandaff. It was written in about 1120 although parts of it were written much earlier. It contains records covering 500 years of the history of the early church there, including a biography of St Teilo. The only reminder of the early Christian church at Llandaff is a late 10th century wheel-headed pillar cross discovered in 1870 in the wall of a well.

Dear God, please can you invent a machine so I don't have to write everything down.

← Extract from Book of Llandaff

SPOT THIS!

Can you find the wheel-headed pillar cross in Llandaff Cathedral? Hint: it's in the south of the cathedral.

Conquering Cardiff

The camp is buzzing with the news. But no word has reached the peasant farmer from Roath, making his regular delivery to the castle. Armed soldiers eye him and his wife with suspicion at the city gate. The wife trembles as the guard in charge inspects their bags. He waves them away. 'The Lord has no need of your provisions today, peasant. Have you not heard? Ivor the Little has raided the castle!'

Ifor Bach now lives here. He is a man of great power.

But not height – ha ha ha!

The Welsh call him Ifor Bach and the Normans call him Ivor the Little.

Rebuilding the Castle

Robert Fitzhamon was one of William the Conqueror's Norman barons in charge of defending the border with Wales. After defeating Iestyn ap Gwrgan, the last native prince of Morgannwg (Glamorgan), he set about rebuilding the abandoned Roman fort. A deep circular ditch was dug and the waste soil used to build a mound, or motte, 8 metres high. On top of this, a wooden tower, or keep, was constructed as the strong point of the castle. A drawbridge, which could be removed in times of danger, joined the motte to the rest of the old Roman fort.

But the Normans weren't safe for long! Sixty years later the Welsh Lord, Ifor Bach, furious with the Normans for taking some of his land in Whitchurch and Rhiwbina, scaled the walls of the castle in the dead of night. He overcame 120 soldiers and archers and took William Earl of Gloucester and his family captive. He released them later but not before he had forced William to restore everything he had taken from him!

Ifor Bach scaled the walls of Cardiff Castle using his bare hands!

...ABOUT 1093 ROBERT FITZHAMON ARRIVES IN CARDIFF...

How do we know?

Records for this period are quite scarce and not all reliable. One account of the Norman campaign in Cardiff – The Winning of Glamorgan – was not written until the 16th century, 500 years later. Because it was loosely based on tales passed down by Welsh storytellers, it is unlikely to be accurate. But it does provide a rich source of information about the local lords and their families and the areas of land allocated to them by Robert Fitzhamon.

A more reliable source of the time is thought to be the account of Giraldus Cambrensis. Writing in 1188 he described the 'extraordinary circumstance' of the capture of the castle by 'Ivor the Little, a man of short stature but of great courage'.

Another clue to the existence of the Normans in Cardiff is a coin bearing William I's inscription found within the castle grounds. The discovery of the coin suggests that William I passed through Cardiff on his return pilgrimage from St David's, in Pembrokeshire.

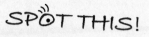 SPOT THIS!

If you climb to the top of the Keep what other buildings in Cardiff can you recognise?

One page down, only 10,342 to go!

Coin found in Cardiff Castle with William I's face on it.

Giraldus Cambrensis wrote in Latin of the relationship between Wales and England.

Life in the Middle Ages

The traveller heads south. His crops are ruined and now that the mill has burned down and all his family with it, what has he to lose? Past the ruined castle at Treoda he crosses the fields to the muddy Roman road. There is space and safety in Cardiff. That much he knows from Llywelyn Bren's men. If he can only persuade the watchkeeper at the North Gate to grant him entry. Otherwise he will have to take his chance crossing the Taff. There's no wall there. With any luck he will be in by nightfall.

Medieval Cardiff

> A house made of straw and animal poo? Sounds like a palace!

Cardiff was formed around the Taff, Ely and Rhymney rivers. This allowed the local people to control trade and keep an eye on who moved along these rivers. The land within this area was mainly fields and the borough of Cardiff itself no more than a small walled town.

The town was surrounded by a ditch, a bank of earth and wooden fences. But to make it more secure, by the 14th century these had been replaced by stone walls. Cardiff's Town Hall was built in High Street in 1338. It measured just 14 x 8 metres and had a meat market next door and the town prison underneath. It was in use for some 400 years.

People lived in thatched-roof houses, made of wood, wattle (woven twigs and branches) and daub (sticky material). An area of Cathays now covered by Colum Road was known as the 'Daubyng Pits'. It provided townspeople with clay which they would mix with straw and animal dung to build the walls of their homes.

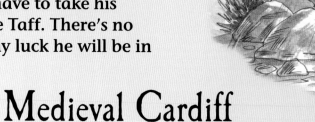

SPOT THIS!

A section of medieval wall survives today. See if you can find it. Psst: look across from the Castle and it's behind the Sony Centre.

TUDOR
1485-1603

STUART
1603-1714

GEORGIAN
1714-1837

VICTORIAN
1837-1901

MODERN
TIMES
1902-
NOW

Cardiff Under Attack

As well as Roath, the lords of Cardiff established manors at Leckwith and Whitchurch. The other land was kept as pasture for grazing. The Welsh lord, Llewelyn Bren, was bailiff at Whitchurch. After falling out with the English lords, he led a revolt in 1316 challenging English rule during the reign of Edward II. Cardiff was attacked and badly damaged. He was later hanged at Cardiff Castle in 1318 by Hugh Despenser and buried at Greyfriars Church.

There were other Welsh attacks on Cardiff. In 1404, Owain Glyndwr, a Welsh ruler, broke through the West Gate, attacked and captured the castle, and set fire to the town. The final defeat of Owain Glyndwr saw a period of peace. Richard Beauchamp, Earl of Warwick, set to restoring the castle and built the octagonal tower to protect the castle's West Gate in 1423. The tower is now known as Beauchamp's tower.

Beauchamp's tower had a spire added in the 19th century.

Llewelyn Bren was a descendant of Ifor Bach. Ifor Bach was his great-great-grandfather.

Openings at the top of Beauchamp's tower meant stones could be dropped on attackers!

How do we know?

How do we know what the borough of Cardiff looked like in the 14th and 15th centuries? There was no description of Cardiff available until the 16th century when John Leland wrote his 'Itinerary of Wales 1536-39', giving a vivid description of its main features. Forty years later Rice Merrick, a notable local historian, carried out a much more detailed study in his 'Booke of Glamorganshire Antiquities'.

Rice Merrick described the Town Hall as: 'a faire Town Hall, wherein is holden the Towne Court, every ffortnight. Adjoining to the same, is a faire Shambles (meat market) below, wherein Victualls are sould: and above, a faire Great Chamber, wherein ye Aldermen and Magistrates vse to consult: and under the Hall is the Prison, wherein offenders and misdoers are committed.'

Although it is written in old English it gives us a vivid picture of what went on in the Town Hall and the building attached to it. How do you think this compares with the activities that take place in our City Hall today?

Faith Under Fire!

Their heads bowed, the faces of the friars are etched with fear as the bell tolls summoning them into the presence of the King's Visitor. Only twelve days have passed since the death of their beloved Prior and now this! The deed of surrender is produced by the servant. A sharp intake of breath from one, a muffled sob from another. Then beneath the King's crest and seal, all meekly sign, surrendering their home. The mourning will go on.

End of the Friaries

Friars were members of the Roman Catholic religious order. They preached their faith and took a vow of poverty.

Around 1530, Henry VIII fell out badly with the Catholic Pope over his divorce from the queen, Catherine of Aragon. Henry declared himself Head of the Church of England and decided to shut down all the religious houses and seize their land and valuable possessions to raise money for his wars with France. This became known as the 'Dissolution of the Monasteries'.

There were two friaries in Cardiff. The Dominicans, known as Blackfriars because of their black cloaks, lived near the Taff Bridge. The Franciscans, who wore rough tunics of greyish-brown, were called Greyfriars. The road where their friary used to stand is named after them.

In 1538, Henry VIII sent Richard Ingworth to Cardiff to force the friars to surrender their buildings to the Crown. Once the buildings had been stripped, local people were quick to help themselves to the stone and timber to improve their own homes. As a result, the friaries fell into ruin. For the friars this meant the loss of their home and their way of life. Some became priests or tutors but many had to accept other work. Older friars would probably have ended their lives begging on the streets.

I married six times! Not bad for someone who looks so grumpy!

Portrait of King Henry VIII

Religious Martyrs

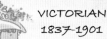

Why do they keep burning these martyrs? I have a perfectly good axe!

In Tudor times people's religious beliefs were determined by the state. Those who didn't fall in line with the laws on religion were often severely punished. After Henry VIII's break with the Pope there was a swing to the Protestant religion, and then back again to Catholicism for a short time under his daughter Mary Tudor. During these confusing years two martyrs were sacrificed in Cardiff for their religious beliefs. Thomas Capper was the first of these. In 1542, after spending 130 days in the town gaol (prison), he was burnt at the stake for the crime of 'heresy', meaning his religious views were different from the State's.

But the most famous Protestant martyr was a fisherman called Rawlins White. He arrived in Cardiff from Somerset in the reign of Mary Tudor and began preaching the gospel throughout Cardiff and nearby villages. This was contrary to the new laws passed during the reign of 'Bloody' Mary which restored the Catholic religion to Britain. By 1555, Protestants were being treated very harshly indeed. When White refused to give up his faith he was imprisoned and later burnt at the stake, most likely at the junction of Church Street and High Street. A plaque was later erected to his memory in the old Bethany Chapel, St Mary Street, where Howells Department Store now stands.

Remains of site of Blackfriars.

SPOT THIS!

Can you find the Rawlins White plaque? Here's a clue: look in the Men's Department of Howells of Cardiff. What is the inscription on the plaque? When was it erected?

CELT
500 BC

ROMAN
AD 43-410

ANGLO-SAXON
AD 450-1066

VIKING
AD 865-1066

MEDIEV
TIME
1066-1

These are the imaginary thoughts of Richard Roberts, an apothecary's assistant at the Blackfriars. He has just lost his home and his job. What does it tell you about the future he is facing? From what you know about life in Tudor Cardiff what are the dangers he will have to overcome?

If I get caught the King's men will barbeque me!

Our second night in the woods. It's not yet autumn so the nights are still warm. But winter will soon be upon us. Where will we sleep then? After the King's Visitor and his men had left, loaded up with our possessions, we fled. Rumour was things might turn nasty with some of the local folk coming to plunder the garden produce and timber. The King's men took everything we had – the goat and cow (a good milker she was), pans and dishes, the kettle, even our small store of corn. Brother John said it was only a matter of time before they pulled out the bells and treasures from the church. The King will have it all for his treasury so they say.

It's safer here but we'll have to return to the town soon. How else will we buy food? And what about money? We will be no better than those poor souls gathering each day at the gates hoping for leftovers. I have skills making up medicines and potions – Brother Michael the apothecary taught me well. But he is old now and cannot walk far. I managed to hide some herbs and oils in the pockets of my cloak. I hope to sell them at the market and use the money to buy bread and ale for us, maybe a few vegetables. With God's help we will survive.

Here are some old apothecary bottles. Some apothecaries were known to accept special requests for poison!

John Speed's plan of Cardiff, 1610

How do we know?

There were no photos in Tudor times so we have to rely on paintings and written accounts from the period. A document called the Augmentation Proceedings of 1540 describes the events which took place when Richard Ingworth forced the seven remaining monks from the Blackfriars, near Taff Bridge, to surrender their property to the Crown. It records the names of the friars and the property confiscated, which included blue vestments (clothes), a pair of organs, ladders and a list of kitchen utensils.

In 1610, cartographer John Speed produced a map of Cardiff and Llandaff. It gives us some idea of the size and shape of the Greyfriars. Next to Cardiff Castle it was the largest dwelling in the town at that time. Greyfriars was excavated by the Marquis of Bute but eventually pulled down in the 1970s to make way for a multi-storey office block. The Capital Tower office block now stands there. The Blackfriars site survives in Bute Park.

John Dane's account in Foxe's Book of Martyrs gives a detailed record of what happened to Rawlins White from his conversion experience to his arrest and imprisonment and eventual burning at the stake.

CARDYFE

A. Smithes stret
B. Shomakers stret
C. West Stret
D. Back stret
E. Hunmanbye stret
F. S. Iohns stret
G. High stret
H. North stret
K. Working stret
L. Porrag stret
M. Frogg Lane
N. st Iohns Church
O. Castell Lane
P. Towne howse
Q. Duke Stret
R. The pootes Releife

Nowe, after he had thus continued as prisoner in Cockmarell Prison at Cardiffe (as is aforesayd) a good space, about three weekes before the daye wherein he suffered, the head Officers of the Towne that had the charge of his execution, were determined to burne hym, because they woulde be the sooner ryd of hym: hauyng not in deede a Writ of execution awarded, as by the law they should haue.

Extract from Foxe's Book of Martyrs. See how the spelling and writing is different in Tudor times!

Rich and Poor

Threads of orange streak the sky as Cardiff comes to life. The driver's cart creaks as he leans forwards, urging the horses up the hill. The stench rising up from the Taff riverside dwellings forces him to cover his nose. Fourteen to a room they say, and with no privy. Soon his load of 'black gold' will be tumbling into the coal cellars of the largest dwelling this side of the Welsh border. If the maid at the castle is to be believed, now that Mr Burges has finished his work, there are enough rooms for every member of the Bute family to have ten apiece if they wished!

In 1870, 3 million tons of coal was shipped out of Cardiff docks. That's the same as 400,000 double decker buses!

You could have swimming lessons at the Turkish Baths in Guildford Crescent. The baths closed in 1984.

Changes for the Better

Cardiff was overcrowded and very dirty. People were often sick and some even died from the poor living conditions. But things started to improve after 1850. Sewers were constructed and a pumping station in Ely gave Cardiff a pure piped water supply. In 1873 public baths and wash houses were built at Guildford Crescent and all new houses had to have a proper toilet. Later, gas and electricity began to be provided. Services were introduced for the collection of rubbish, and streets were cleaned and lit by gas lamps. As a result the death rate in Cardiff fell by half.

Hear all about it! New school opens in Cardiff!

There were few schools at this time and only 1 in 3 children had a primary education. After the Education Act of 1870, new schools were opened, including the Wesleyan. By the end of the century, another twenty had been added, including Albany, Radnor and Severn Road. Classes were often overcrowded. Children were in danger too from the coal fires that heated the classrooms. After 1885 secondary education started to be provided but only children whose parents could afford the school fees benefitted. Most children at the end of the 19th century could expect to spend their teenage years doing hard physical work. Girls often found work as servants in wealthy homes and boys would end up as street sweepers or labourers.

The new Wesleyan Sunday School, which has been in course of erection for some months past in Charles street, Cardiff, was opened on Wednesday. The building possesses a handsome exterior... The school is planned to accommodate 600 children...

Here's an extract from the Western Mail 1875 – reporting on the opening of the Wesleyan School.

Cardiff Castle Restored

Just a short distance from some of the worst slums in Cardiff, life at the Castle was very different. Over the centuries it was owned by a number of noble families. By 1776, it had come into the possession of the very rich Bute family. The 3rd Marquis of Bute, who was considered one of the wealthiest men in Britain at the time, had a keen interest in art and archaeology. In 1865 he employed an architect named William Burges to start the work of restoring the Castle. Great care was taken to preserve the original Roman Wall and the Norman Keep.

John Crichton-Stuart, 3rd Marquis of Bute

SPOT THIS!

How many different types of animals are sitting on the Animal Wall surrounding the Castle?

Special workshops were erected and the finest craftsmen employed to produce stained-glass windows and medieval Gothic-style decoration, such as the famous Animal Wall. Three new towers were added to the existing castle buildings – the Clock Tower, decorated with the Bute family coat-of-arms; the Bute Tower, topped with a roof garden; the third, the Guest Tower had rooms for the servants as well as visitors. It also had a children's nursery decorated with pictures from fairy tales, and even a skittle alley!

Read this imaginary letter, based on facts, that Gwyneth, a kitchen maid at Cardiff Castle, has written home. She has only been working at the Castle for a week. What does it tell you about life at the Castle for the servants and for the Bute family? How different would it have been from Gwyneth's life at home?

JOHN III MARQUESS OF BUTE

Dear Mam

It was hard leaving you at the station last Monday but I am settling in. My room is in the Clock Tower and I've had trouble getting to sleep because of the clock chiming. I start work at 6.30 every day. First I have to light the stove (there are six ovens!) then grind the coffee beans. After that I lay out all the knives and dishes for Cook to prepare breakfast for the family. They have four meals a day and all on silver platters. At 7.30 they have their tea, but they call it dinner. Six courses every evening!

The hardest job is cleaning the copper pans. Some of them are big enough to sit in! Cook showed me how to mix a paste of flour, vinegar and fine sand and to rub it in with the palm of my hand. The pots come up shiny but it makes my arms ache.

Every afternoon I have two hours off. Yesterday Elizabeth, another maid, showed me the castle grounds. Two footmen followed us but Cook soon sent them packing. Mixing with the male servants is strictly forbidden! I won't be able to come home much as I only have one day off a week. I miss you and Dadda but don't worry about me. People are kind here and though I only see Lord and Lady Bute from a distance I hear they treat their servants well.

With love,
Gwyneth

It was 'ard being a maid for the master but he was very kind.

The Marquis of Bute was only 21 when he started the transformation of Cardiff Castle with William Burges.

How do we know?

The Victorians were great recorders of their time and have left us many interesting and detailed accounts of what life was like for both rich and poor people. We know how dreadful the living conditions were in the mid-nineteenth century from a report written by a Health Inspector called T.W. Rammell who visited Cardiff in 1849. He vividly describes the dreadful living conditions of people forced, because of their poverty, to live in tightly packed slum dwellings in Stanley Street (near where the Cardiff International Arena now stands). With nowhere to wash themselves or their clothes, and with heaps of decayed vegetable matter in the street in front of the house, it's not hard to understand why Rammell commented, 'The smell arising was most overpowering.'

What a contrast with life in the 3rd Marquis of Bute's Castle! Pictures and early photographs from that time show how much the Castle had changed after its restoration by William Burges. Further to the left of the Clock Tower is the octagonal Beauchamp Tower, originally built in 1423, but now topped by Burges with a wooden Gothic spire.

William Burges decorated the Clock Tower with figures of Roman gods and shields of the Bute family above.

Crossing the Centuries

The street cleaners have been out early. Strips of red, white and blue bunting flutter to transform the drab docks for the day. An important-looking man in a top hat and black tailcoat stands to attention. Behind him the choir bursts into song: 'Hen Wlad fy Nhadau.' Clapping breaks out as crowds strain to watch the royal carriage coming into view. Then, a young girl, pretty in pink, steps forward and curtsies, her head dipped. It is 1907, and King Edward VII and Queen Alexandra have arrived to open the new Queen Alexandra Dock.

The Pierhead building, built in 1897, was the headquarters of the Bute Dock Company. Today, it is part of the National Assembly of Wales.

He was the Prince of Wales, but now he's the King of the United Kingdom!

Queen Alexandra was a keen photographer.

King Coal

In 1839, the 2nd Marquis of Bute had built the first dock in Cardiff, the Bute Docks. He did this to export the increasing amounts of iron and coal coming down from the South Wales valleys. Two million tons of coal were carried by steamship around the world from Cardiff docks in one year. The world's first £1 million deal was signed at the Coal Exchange in Mount Stuart Square in 1901.

By 1913, Cardiff was exporting more coal than any other dock in the world. Coal was bringing huge wealth to Cardiff for the dock owners and mine owners. Some of them used their wealth to build large homes for themselves. Ely Court, now known as Insole House, was built by James Harvey Insole, a colliery owner.

Bute Dock Offices, Cardiff

...1894 ROATH PARK BUILT...1902 TRAMS IN QUEEN STREET...

Population Explosion!

As exports of iron and coal grew, so did the number of people living in Cardiff. In 1871 the population was about 40,000. By 1901 it had more than quadrupled to 164,000! Workers moved up from Somerset and Devon to find work as bricklayers and carpenters on the new houses being built in streets off Whitchurch Road and Crwys Road in Cathays. Outlying parts of Cardiff were growing rapidly too. Farms such as the Grange, Splott and Penylan gave their names to new suburbs.

Many people travelled much further to settle in Cardiff. Dockworkers and sailors from across the world moved into an area near the docks. This area became known as Tiger Bay. Was it named after a music-hall song of the 1860s or because Portuguese seamen said sailing in Cardiff was like sailing into a bay of tigers? No one knows for sure! What is certain is that over 50 different nationalities grew up in that neighbourhood, making it Wales's oldest multi-ethnic community.

Cardiff was officially declared a city in 1905!

Leisure Time

With more people earning more money, new shops opened in St Mary Street and The Hayes, while arcades such as the Royal and Morgan arcades allowed people to shop in comfort. The working week was shortened giving people from Saturday lunchtime and all of Sunday for leisure. Theatres and concert halls sprang up including the Park Hall in Park Place. The New Theatre opened and that Christmas the first of its annual pantomimes was performed. Cinemas such as the Picture Playhouse in Queen Street and the Gaiety in City Road drew in crowds for the silent movies. Outside the city centre, Roath Park and its newly created lake opened in 1894.

From 1902, people could ride the electric trams from Roath Park through busy St Mary Street.

SPOT THIS!

The exact year the New Theatre was opened is on the building. Can you spot it? Psst: look up.

Read this imaginary diary entry, based on a real event, written by Gwendoline Evans, an 11-year-old pupil at the expensive Howells School in Llandaff. Her father owns one of the huge steamships which carries coal and iron to Argentina and other distant lands.

This photograph of Roath Park was taken in 1920. How has it changed today?

The Bandstand Roath Park, Cardiff. 6090.

Saturday, 13th July 1907

It has been such a special day that I will never forget if I live to be 100! Papa took me to the opening of the new Queen Alexandra Dock and told me he had a day of treats in store for me! He had to write a letter to the headmistress excusing me from school for the day. I feel very privileged to have a school place at Howells, but I did not care for the stiff expression on Miss Syms' face when she said I should not let being presented to royalty 'go to my head'.
 The King and Queen came specially from London. Her Majesty looked so splendid in her long cream gown and wide-brimmed hat. I was chosen to present her with a small bouquet. I practised my curtsey over and over but still I felt very nervous. After the ceremony which was a little tedious and long, there was a magnificent lunch at the new City Hall.

In the afternoon we took the tram to Roath Park and went boating on the lake. The weather was so warm Papa took off his jacket to row and at the end was quite pink from his exertions. As we drove home I expected a quiet supper. But Papa produced tickets for the New Theatre and we spent the evening watching Mr Harry Houdini perform his amazing stunts and magic tricks!

I gave Queen Alexandra some flowers too – she is really pretty!

UDOR 1485-1603

STUART 1603-1714

GEORGIAN 1714-1837

VICTORIAN 1837-1901

MODERN TIMES
1902-NOW

← The Morgan Arcade was built in 1896.
You can still see some of the original
wood and brass shop fronts today.

How do we know?

Photography had just been invented
in Victorian times, with the first
photographs being taken in the
1830s. The BBC now holds photos
of the opening of the Queen
Alexandra Dock in 1907 by King
Edward VII and Queen Alexandra
after whom the dock was named.
Look at the photograph of
Queen Alexandra below. People had
to stand still for a long time otherwise
the picture would be blurred. Photos are
also a great way of seeing how people and
places have changed through the years. Look
at the clothes that people are wearing in
Roath Park on the
left-hand page.
How has clothing
changed? And if
you walk through
the Morgan
Arcade today,
how do you
think the shops
have changed?

Smile, Your Majesty!

I am smiling!

Queen Alexandra's interest
in photography helped to
popularise it as a hobby. →

25

A City at War

Mam has been trying to hide her tears all morning. Our brother, Gareth, has been called to fight the war against Germany. We go to wave him off from Cardiff Central. Other lads have gone from our street although Dad, who fought in France in the First World War, has signed up for the Home Guard. The trains seem to be taking our men on a weekly basis. I'm trying to be brave but it's hard as I don't know if Gareth will ever come back.

Bombs Over Cardiff

When Britain declared war on Germany in 1939, Cardiff was a city of over 250,000. An impressive new civic centre had been built, including the City Hall, the National Museum of Wales and the War Memorial in Alexandra Gardens. By 1941, Britain was in the middle of the Blitz. Hundreds of Cardiff children were evacuated to safer parts of Wales while those who stayed had to attend air-raid practice at school.

TAKE COVER

1941, Neville Street after a raid in the Second World War.

In 1955, 10 years after the war ended in 1945, Cardiff became the capital city of Wales.

Cardiff's huge docks and its coal industry made it a prime target. The worst air raid hit in January 1941 when buildings in Canton, Grangetown and Riverside were badly hit. Canton High School was partially destroyed but in keeping with the wartime spirit children continued their classes in the local library and the Methodist Church Hall. Llandaff Cathedral was another casualty that night, shattered by a landmine. When the 'all clear' sounded in the early hours of the following morning, more than 150 people had died and many more were left with serious injuries.

Life in Wartime Cardiff

> I hope somebody nice picks us.

People had to change the way they lived to survive in wartime Cardiff. Gasmasks had to be carried everywhere and gas-mask drills became part of school life. Bomb shelters were built and even Llandaff Church School had a red brick shelter built in the playground. Women replaced men in factories and families became actively involved, volunteering as Air Raid Wardens, Fire Watchers and many women joined the Land Army.

Food, clothing, footwear and even petrol became rationed. People were given ration books to make sure that they had a fair share of the foods that were hard to obtain, such as meat, eggs and sugar. Parks and gardens were turned into allotments so that people could 'Dig for Victory' and grow their own food. Scrap metal and park railings were collected at 'Metal for Munitions' dumps to turn into guns and ammunition.

Extract from 'Cardiff Schools and the age of the Second World War', 6th January 1941

Across the City attendance is down. Only 57% of the girls at Severn Road Girls School attend, many children having been rendered homeless through Thursday's Fire Blitz. At Albany Road Boys School, the attendance is very low, in consequence of the evacuation of many families from their houses which were utterly or partially demolished by bombs... It was the most destructive and widespread raid we have experienced up to date.

How do we know?

There is no shortage of evidence for what took place in Cardiff in the twentieth century. We have photos, films, numerous detailed written accounts and of course the stories of people still living who experienced the events first hand.

The photo of Neville Street gives us some idea of the devastation caused by the German bombing in 1941. There are also written records from a number of Cardiff schools. These provide us with a clear picture of how buildings were damaged, how many children were able to attend school after the bombings and the names of teachers and pupils who were killed.

SPOT THIS!

What are the words inscribed on the National War Memorial in Cathays Park?

CELT
500 BC

ROMAN
AD 43-410

ANGLO-
SAXON
AD 450-
1066

VIKING
AD 865-
1066

MEDIE
TIM
1066-

Cardiff Today and Tomorrow...

Today, Cardiff has a population of 328,000 and attracts more than 12 million tourists every year. It hosts some of the most impressive buildings of modern-day architecture. We know all about Cardiff's past from things people have left behind, such as written accounts, artefacts and buildings. But what about Cardiff today? What will we leave for our children and our children's children to discover?

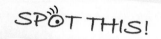

SPOT THIS!

In 2005, to celebrate 100 years of city status, Cardiff established a centenary walk. The walk is 3.5 km in total and shows 41 of Cardiff's most celebrated landmarks. Will these waymarkers leave clues in our roads and on our pavements for future archaeologists to find?

The Welsh flag was granted official status in 1959. The origin of the dragon is lost in legend. Wales and Bhutan are the only two countries to have dragons on their flags.

Cardiff is one of the flattest cities in Britain and has more hours of sunlight than Milan!

Spillers Records was founded in 1894 by Henry Spiller. It's the world's oldest record shop. Will music shops be a thing of the past as more and more people buy online?

The Millennium Stadium has hosted some of the biggest pop concerts and sporting events, including Madonna and two Rugby World Cups, with the Final in 1999! Will future generations still use this venue and what kinds of entertainment will they be watching?

The Wales Millennium Centre opened in 2004. The Centre is recognised as one of the world's leading centres for the performing arts. The amazing exterior has featured in Dr Who and Torchwood.

There's a whole floor at the library just for kids!

Cardiff Central Library is one of the city's most energy efficient buildings. It has six floors and three restaurants. Will future generations still be using libraries or will everything be online?

Cardiff Castle has become one of the world's most famous castles and boasts 2,000 years of history. Will it still be standing in another 2,000 years?

How will they know?

We only have to click onto the Internet to find proof of how we live our lives. We download pictures, keep blogs and send emails. Will the Internet act as a museum in the future? Should we still keep artefacts for future generations to see and touch? How much of today's Cardiff will still exist in 10, 100 or 1,000 years' time?

Glossary

AD – a short way of writing the Latin words anno Domini, which mean 'in the year of our Lord' i.e. after the birth of Christ.

Apothecary – an old-fashioned word for a chemist.

Archaeology – the study of past human life.

Artefact – another word for an object, often an archaeological one.

Barracks – a building where soldiers stay.

Caer Taff – this means 'fort by the river'. Many historians believe this may be how Cardiff got its name.

Cartographer – someone who draws maps.

Catholicism – a Christian religion, headed by the Pope.

Christianity – the Christian religion, which believes Christ is the son of God.

Church of England – a Christian religion, headed by the king or queen.

Excavate – to dig up buried objects in order to find out about the past.

Fire Watcher – during the Second World War, bombs caused fires. People were needed to look out for them to alert the fire brigade so the fires could be put out before they spread.

Friars – members of the Roman Catholic religion who lived together in a friary.

Glamorgan – also known as Morgannwg.

Home Guard – part-time volunteers who wanted to help protect Britain during the Second World War.

Martyr – someone prepared to die for their beliefs, usually their religion.

Medieval – a period of time in the Middle Ages: roughly from AD 1000 to the 15th century.

Mill – a building, like a factory, with machinery for producing goods such as flour or material for clothes.

Monastery – a place where monks live and worship.

Pagan – someone who believes in lots of different gods rather than just one.

Pedlar – someone who travels the country selling things.

Pope – the head of the Roman Catholic Church.

Prior – the deputy head of a monastery (the Abbot is the head).

Privy – old-fashioned name for toilet.

Protestant – one kind of Christian who does not follow Roman Catholic beliefs.

Ration Book – during the Second World War, certain food had to be rationed. Your Ration Book showed how much of this food you could have every week.

Roman Catholic – a member of the Christian religion which considers the Pope to be the head of its church.

Silures – a Celtic tribe that ruled Cardiff before the Romans.

Slum – a very poor part of a city that's rundown, dirty and overcrowded with people.

...1912 Cardiff City won the Welsh Cup for the first time...

Index

...1949 THE FIRST WELSH-LANGUAGE PRIMARY SCHOOL IN CARDIFF WAS OPENED...

31

Acknowledgements

The author and publishers would like to thank the following people for their generous help:
Claire Hamer at Cardiff Castle; Kay Kays at the National Museum of Wales;
Matthew Witty – www.cardiffians.co.uk for all his help and images and
Louise Cordery at Glamorgan Archives

The publishers would like to thank the following people and organizations
for their permission to reproduce material on the following pages:

Front cover: Christopher Dodge/shutterstock; p7: Crown copyright: Royal Commission on the Ancient
and Historical Monuments of Wales, Cardiff Museum; p9: The National Library of Wales; p11: Classical
Numismatic Group, Inc. www.cngcoins.com; p16: Terence Mendoza/shutterstock; p17: Glamorgan Archives;
p18: Matthew Witty – www.cardiffians.co.uk; p22: www.rhiw.com; p23: Cardiff Central Library/Local studies;
p24: Matthew Witty – www.cardiffians.co.uk; p25: World History Archive / Alamy; p26: Matthew Witty –
www.cardiffians.co.uk

All other images copyright of Hometown World

Written by Sue Barrow
Educational consultant: Neil Thompson
Local history consultants: Dennis Morgan
Designed by Stephen Prosser

Illustrated by Kate Davies, Virginia Gray, Peter Kent and John MacGregor
Additional photographs by Alex Long

First published by HOMETOWN WORLD in 2010
Hometown World Ltd
7 Northumberland Buildings
Bath BA1 2JB

www.hometownworld.co.uk

ISBN 978-1-84993-002-4

Your past
Your now
Your future

Your history4ever

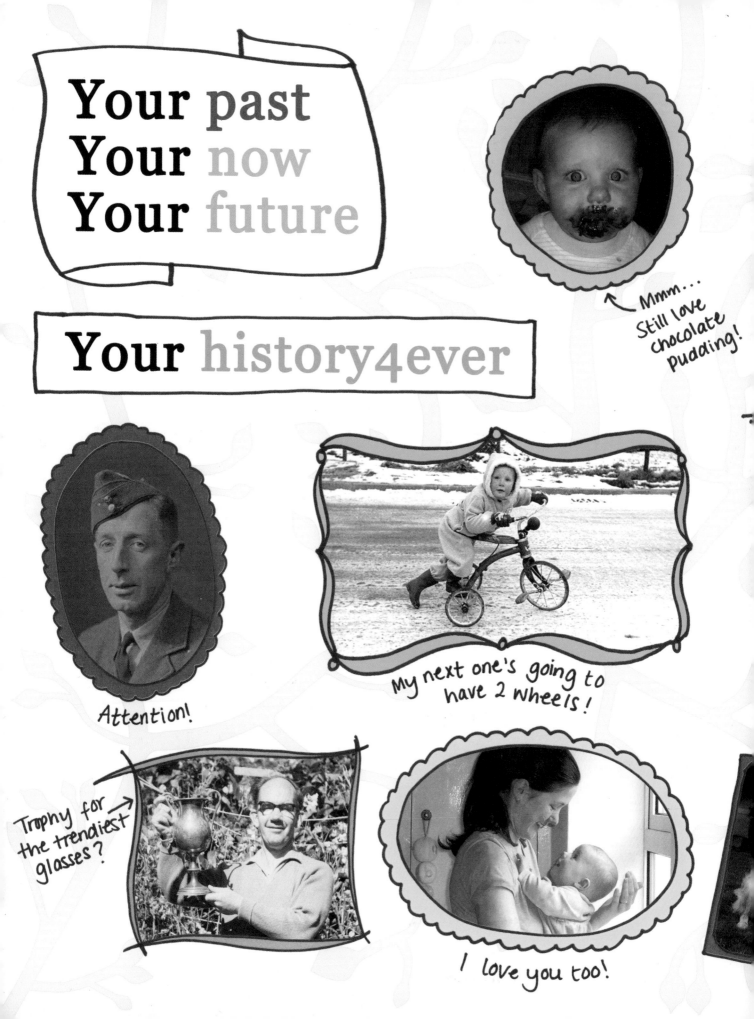

Mmm... Still love chocolate pudding!

Attention!

My next one's going to have 2 wheels!

Trophy for the trendiest glasses?

I love you too!